Ways into Technology

On Wheels

Written by Richard & Louise Spilsbury

W

FRANKLIN WATTS

LONDON·SYDNEY

This edition 2012

First published in 2008 by Franklin Watts
338 Euston Road
London NW1 3BH

Franklin Watts Australia
Level 17/207 Kent Street
Sydney NSW 2000

Copyright © Franklin Watts 2008

Editor: Julia Bird
Design: Shobha Mucha
Photography: Paul Bricknell (unless
otherwise credited)
Consultant: Pam Bolton, design and technology adviser

A CIP catalogue record for this book
is available from the British Library

ISBN 978 1 4451 0959 6

Dewey Classification 621.8'11

Printed in China

Picture credits: p.6: (top) istockphoto © Stane Crnjak; (bottom)
istockphoto © Tony Tremblay; p.7 (top) Shutterstock © Timothy Large;
(bottom) Alamy © David Stares; p.8: Shutterstock © Jane McIlroy; p.9:
(top) istockphoto © Sabina Salihbasic; (bottom) istockphoto © Evrim Sen;
p.10: Shutterstock © Patrick Laverdent; p.14: (bottom left) istockphoto ©
Jason Lugo; (bottom right) © objectsforall; p.16: © Nic Randall/Alamy;
p.20: istockphoto © Mark Evans; p.21: (top) Shutterstock © iofoto;
(middle) Shutterstock © Nigel Carse; (bottom) Shutterstock © Emin
Kuliyev; p.26: Shutterstock © Tomasz Pietryszek; p.27: (clockwise from
top) Shutterstock © Trutta55; Shutterstock © objectsforall; istockphoto
© Angela Farley; istockphoto © Judi Ashlock; istockphoto © Kenneth C.
Zirkel; istockphoto © Adam Korzekwa.

Every attempt has been made to clear copyright. Should there be any
inadvertent omission please apply to the publisher for rectification.

Thanks to our models: Tilly Lumsden, Amrit Paul,
Phoebe Price and Louis Szopinski.

Franklin Watts is a division of Hachette Children's Books,
an Hachette Livre UK company.
www.hachette.co.uk

Contents

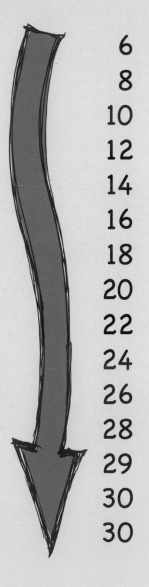

Wheels everywhere

Wheels make things move. The wheels on vehicles help them carry people and things from place to place.

This is a motorbike. It carries one or two people.

Removal vans are big so they can carry furniture.

This is a
police car.
What does
it do?

What is the
name of this
vehicle?

What
does it
carry?

What other kinds of
vehicles can you name?

7

Different parts

This is an old, vintage car. The parts of the car are labelled. The chassis is the frame. What are the other parts for?

Steering Wheel

Wing Mirror

Windscreen

Headlights

Chassis

Wheels

How is this car the same as modern cars? How is it different?

Fire engines have flashing parts
that light up and make a noise.

These warn people to get
out of the way when
vehicles have to go fast.

What other vehicles have
flashing lights or sirens? Why?

Wheels go round!

An axle is a round bar that joins wheels. A tractor has an axle that turns. The wheels are attached to the axle, so when the axle turns, the wheels turn too.

Axle

Axle

A car has a fixed axle. The axle stays still and the wheels turn around it.

Amrit tests two different ways of holding axles on a cardboard box chassis.

He sticks triangles of card to the chassis and punches holes through them. He pushes a dowel rod through the two holes and attaches the wheels to it.

Next, Amrit tries gluing on clothes pegs and using these to hold on a dowel and wheels.

Which method would you choose?

A **tipping** trailer

Phoebe is making a trailer to carry a load.

First, she cuts two lengths of dowel using a saw. These will be axles.

She attaches the axles to a cardboard chassis with elastic bands.

Safety note:
Saws are very sharp. An adult must always be present when you are using one.

She slips cotton reels on to the axles and holds them on with Plasticine.

Phoebe sticks a long piece of folded card to the chassis. She tapes a box to the card. The box can tip up now!

She punches a hole in the trailer with a hole punch.

Now she can attach the tractor to a truck with an elastic band.

Toolbox
- Cardboard
- Dowel rods
- Cotton reels
- Junior saw
- Elastic bands
- Small box
- Hole punch
- Plasticine
- Tape • Card

stop and go

Amrit pushes this car to make it move. Pushes and pulls are forces.

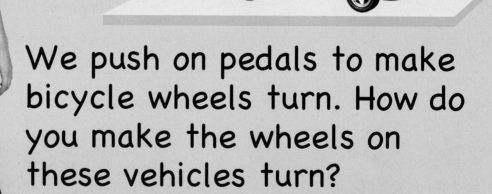

We push on pedals to make bicycle wheels turn. How do you make the wheels on these vehicles turn?

Forces make vehicles stop, go, speed up and slow down.

What will happen if Amrit pushes the car harder? How can he stop the car?

What else do forces do to vehicles? Turn the page to find out.

Forces also make vehicles change direction.

When wind blows into the sail of this land yacht, it steers the yacht in that direction.

What will happen when the wind changes direction?

Make your own land yacht! Make a chassis with axles and wheels. Then stick an upright dowel rod to the chassis with Plasticine.

Tie another dowel across the first, using wire or elastic bands.

Tape the end of a square of fabric to the second dowel.

Now tape the other corners of the fabric to the back of the chassis. Try using a hair dryer to make your land yacht move.

Testing cars

Tilly is making a car from a construction kit.

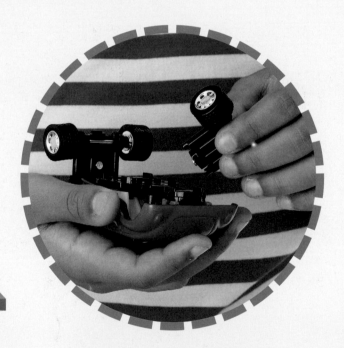

Toolbox
- Construction kit car
- Cardboard • Ruler
- Box or books for ramp

She attaches the wheels and makes sure that the axles turn.

Tilly uses a box to make a ramp and lets the car roll down it.

She predicts how far from the ramp the car will go. Then she tests other toy vehicles.

Prediction

Actual

	My Car	Toy Truck	Toy Fire Engine
60cm			
50cm			
40cm			
30cm			
20cm			
10cm			

What will happen if Tilly makes the ramp steeper?

Who is it for?

When designers plan a new vehicle, they think about who it is for and what loads it will carry.

Designers make computer drawings and models to test their designs.

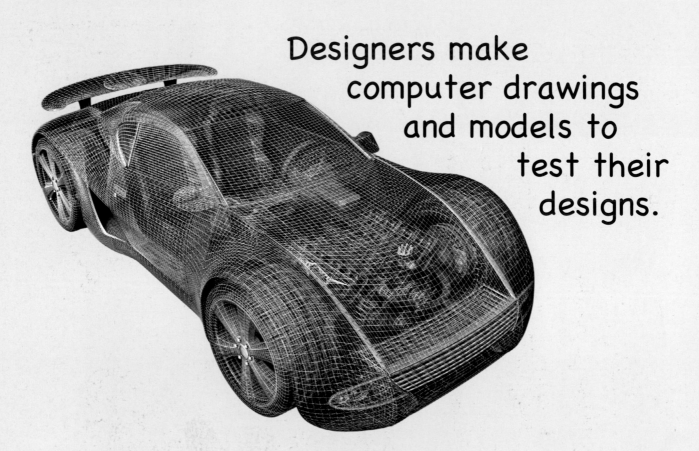

What kind of vehicle do you think this is?

Vehicles are different designs because they have different purposes.

This bicycle has stabilisers to make it safer to ride.

This trolley has high sides to hold shopping.

Who are these vehicles designed for?

Plan a van

Louis decides to make an ice cream van. He looks at the internet for some ideas.

He draws and labels his design.

ice cream

plastic

card-board box

LOUIS' ICE-CREAMS

wheels

Louis wants the van to be colourful to get people's attention. He also plans to have a big side window where ice creams can be served.

What kind of van would you design?

Louis selects materials and tools for the different parts of the van.

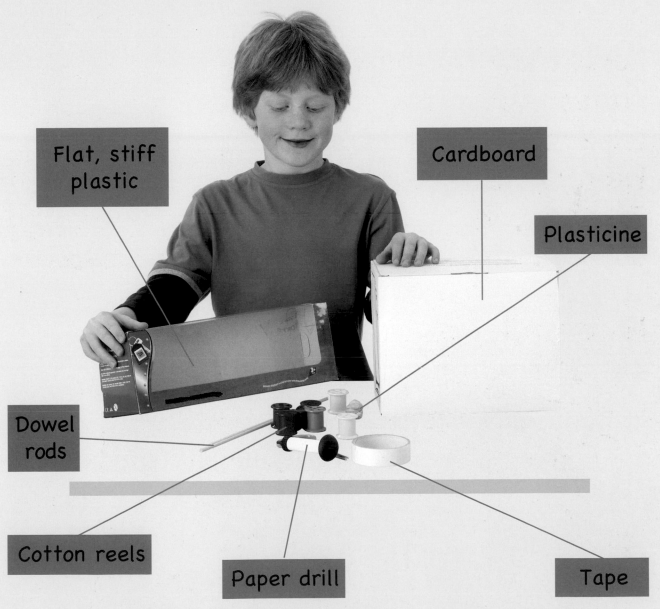

Flat, stiff plastic

Cardboard

Plasticine

Dowel rods

Cotton reels

Paper drill

Tape

What materials does Louis use to make each part of the van? Turn the page to find out.

Make a van

Louis uses the box for the chassis. He draws on the side window and windscreen. He cuts them out with a paper drill and scissors.

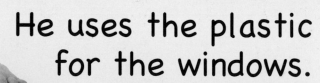

He uses the plastic for the windows. He measures the plastic to make sure it will fit. Then he tapes it in.

Louis tapes on dowel rods as axles. He sticks cotton reels to the rods with Plasticine.

Louis makes a logo out of red paper and an ice-cream cone from brown paper and cotton wool. He sticks them to the van with glue.

Does Louis's model look like his design?

Safety note:
Take care with scissors.

What do you know?

Can you match the names of the car parts with the correct part? For example, A = Windscreen.

Windscreen

Wheels

Headlight

Wing mirror

Chassis

Can you match
each of the
vehicles above
with the load
that it carries?

Useful words

Axle – a long rounded bar that joins a pair of wheels.

Chassis – frame or body of a vehicle.

Design – plan for the way an object will look, what it will be made from and how big it will be.

Direction – the way that a vehicle or person is travelling or looking. You change direction when you turn left from right, or north to south for example.

Dowel – a cylinder-shaped, thin stick of wood.

Force – a push or a pull.

Logo – a sign or name that is linked to a particular company or thing that people buy.

Materials – things we need to make something. Plastic, fabric, metal and wood are all materials.

Predict – suggest what may happen based on information that you have.

Purpose – what something is used for.

Siren – warning signal that is usually a loud wailing sound.

Stabilisers - an extra set of wheels that are attached to a bicycle to make it more stable and easier to ride.

Steer – to control and turn a vehicle to follow a route.

Trailer – a container with wheels that is pulled along by a vehicle like a car or a truck.

Upright - standing up.

Vehicle – vehicles carry people and things from place to place. Vehicles such as cars and buses move on wheels.

Vintage – very old.

Some answers

Here are some answers to the questions we have asked in this book. Don't worry if you had some different answers to ours; you may be right, too. Talk through your answer with other people and see if you can explain why it is right.

Page 7   Police cars carry police officers to where there is trouble. The other vehicle is a post van. It carries letters and parcels. There are lots of other vehicles you could name including a train, wheelbarrow, ice-cream van, bicycle, skateboard, dump truck etc.

Page 8   The steering wheel turns the wheels to change the direction in which the car is going. Windscreens let drivers see the road ahead. Wing mirrors allow drivers to see behind the car. Headlights can light the road ahead when it is dark or foggy. Wheels turn to make the car move. The vintage car is the same as a modern car as it has many of the same parts. It is different to a modern car because it is made from different materials and the chassis is open, with no glass in the windows.

Page 9   Ambulances use lights and sirens too. They need to get people to hospital fast so they warn other vehicles and people to get out of the way quickly. Police cars also have lights and sirens. They help police cars get through traffic quickly to places where there is trouble.

Page 14   We push the handles on a wheelbarrow to make it move. Skateboarders push against the ground with their foot to make the wheels turn.

Page 15   If Amrit pushes the car harder (with more force) it will go faster. To stop the car he could pull on it. A pull is a force in the opposite direction to a push.

Page 16   If the wind changes direction, the yacht will change direction too.

Page 19   If Tilly makes the ramp steeper, the car will travel further from the bottom of the ramp.

Page 20   This is a sports car. It can carry two passengers.

Page 21   The tricycle is for a toddler. The tractor is for a farmer.

Page 26   Windscreen A, wheels B, headlight C, wing mirror D, chassis E.

Page 27   Rubbish bag - rubbish truck, garden waste – wheelbarrow, horse – horsebox.

Index

About this book

Ways into Technology is designed to encourage children to think about the way the things in their world are designed and made. The topic of vehicles is popular for this age group and an easy and familiar one for children to think and talk about.

• Working through this book will introduce the children to some of the concepts and vocabulary, such as purpose, properties and design, linked to design technology. As they work through the activities they will experience different methods of joining materials and gain a little knowledge about simple mechanisms such as hinges and wheels and axles.

• Wheels and axles are an important feature of the vehicles topic at this stage. Children will need lots of chances to explore these, perhaps by taking apart some old toy vehicles and by trying out ways of making them using construction kits such as K'nex.

• There are opportunities to link making vehicles with science and maths, for example when thinking about forces and movement. On pages 16-17 a child tests how far cars travel off a ramp. This is a good maths measuring and estimating exercise but also a chance to explain gravity if children wonder what force is pushing the car down the slope, because all they have to do is let them go to make the cars move. This is also a good chance to discuss what makes a fair test: letting two or more cars go down a slope is a fair way of testing because if you pushed them on a flat surface one person might push harder than the other.